First World War
and Army of Occupation
War Diary
France, Belgium and Germany

15 DIVISION
Headquarters, Branches and Services
General Staff
6 August 1915 - 24 December 1915

WO95/1911/1

The Naval & Military Press Ltd
www.nmarchive.com
Published in association with The National Archives

Published by

The Naval & Military Press Ltd

Unit 10 Ridgewood Industrial Park,

Uckfield, East Sussex,

TN22 5QE England

Tel: +44 (0) 1825 749494

www.naval-military-press.com

www.nmarchive.com

This diary has been reprinted in facsimile from the original. Any imperfections are inevitably reproduced and the quality may fall short of modern type and cartographic standards.

© Crown Copyright
Images reproduced by permission of The National Archives, London, England, 2015.

Contents

Document type	Place/Title	Date From	Date To
Heading	WO95/1911/1 15 Div HQ Gen Staff & Depts Miscellaneous Ops 1915		
Heading	Miscellaneous Operation. 1915		
Miscellaneous	First Army No. 502 (G).	23/12/1915	23/12/1915
Miscellaneous	15th Division.	24/12/1915	24/12/1915
Miscellaneous	56/G IVth Corps. No. 1358 (G)	24/12/1915	24/12/1915
Miscellaneous	Report On Bombing Expedition South Of Mametz (by party of 1st Bn. Cheshire Regiment) on night of 6th/7th December, 1915	06/12/1915	06/12/1915
Map	Sketch Map of bombing expedition south of Mametz 6/7 Dec 1915		
Miscellaneous	Headquarters XV Division.	00/12/1915	00/12/1915
Miscellaneous	1st Army G.S. 232	16/12/1915	16/12/1915
Miscellaneous	Advanced 1st Army. No. 612 (G) 6. 14th December, 1915	14/12/1915	14/12/1915
Miscellaneous	Adv. First Army. O.A. 225	09/12/1915	09/12/1915
Miscellaneous	Summary of small offensive Operation carried out by 6th Battalion Gloucester Regiment (48th Division). on 25th/26th November, 1915	25/11/1915	25/11/1915
Map	Barrage For First Phase "Attack"		
Map	Barrage For Second Phase "Withdrawal"		
Miscellaneous	1st Army No. G.S. 189	07/10/1915	07/10/1915
Miscellaneous	Memorandum on The lessons to be drawn from the recent offensive operations.	05/10/1915	05/10/1915
Miscellaneous	15th Division.	30/08/1915	30/08/1915
Miscellaneous	Extract From Report By G.O.C. 6th Division, In Reply To Questions Asked By 2nd Army.		
Miscellaneous	6th Corps.	14/08/1915	14/08/1915
Miscellaneous	16th Infantry Brigade. Extract From Report On The Operations At Hooge 9th August, 1915	09/08/1915	09/08/1915
Miscellaneous	Extract From 16th Infantry Brigade Operation Order Of 6th August, 1915	06/08/1915	06/08/1915
Miscellaneous	15th Division.	28/08/1915	28/08/1915
Miscellaneous	Extract from memorandum regarding preparations made for operations for the capture of Neuve Chapelle.		

WO95/1911-1

15 Div HQ Gen Staff or Depts

Miscellaneous Ops 1915

W 74—664 250,000 3/15 L.S.& Co.

Army Form W. 3091.

Part of 56/9.

Cover for Documents.

Nature of Enclosures.

Miscellaneous Operations. 1915

Notes, or Letters written.

First Army No. 502(G).

Summary of report on bombing raid carried out by the 4th Battalion Grenadier Guards, 3rd Guards Brigade, on the 11th-12th December against the enemy's trenches to the N.E. of NEUVE CHAPELLE (M.35.d and M.36.c).

---

1. **Preliminary reconnaissance and arrangements.**

   The raid was first considered when patrols reported slackness on the part of the enemy's sentries. A gap which was cut in the enemy's wire was reconnoitred on the 10th December and reported to be open. The party carrying out this reconnaissance consisted of two officers and a sergeant who were to accompany the attacking party and they were instructed to reconnoitre thoroughly the ground between our trenches and the point in the enemy's line to be attacked.

   The officer commanding the company which was to carry out the raid (Captain Sir R. Filmer, Bart., Grenadier Guards) was instructed personally to reconnoitre on the night of the 11th December the point to be attacked. He was to be accompanied by 1 N.C.O. and 3 men and the reconnaissance was to be made after the moon had gone down.

   In the event of the gap being found to be still open the reconnoitring party was to listen carefully for the sound of any movement in the enemy's trench and to locate the positions of his posts or machine guns.

   Having done this the O.C. was to determine the central point of the attack and then to return to our own lines leaving one man to watch the gap and connecting files to guide the attacking party.

   Previous to this the O.C. had explained minutely to the officers and N.C.Os. who were to form the party under his command :-

   (i). The party to which each men was allotted and his duties
   (ii). The plan of attack (which was subject to modification after he had made his reconnaissance).
   (iii). The method of retirement.

2. **Scheme.**

   During the preliminary reconnaissance the party told off to carry out the attack was to assemble in the British front line trenches ready to advance, and was to be composed as follows:-

   Right party   -   (6 bombers.
                     (3 carriers.
                     (2 bayonet men.

   Centre party -   (3 bombers.
                     (2 carriers.
                     (6 bayonet men.

   Left Party   -   (6 bombers.
                     (3 carriers.
                     (2 bayonet men.

   O.C. Bombers -   Lieut. Ponsonby, Grenadier Guards.
   O.C. Assault -   Lieut. Nairn, Grenadier Guards.
   O.C. Attack   -   Capt. Sir R. Filmer, Bt., Grenadier Gds

On

On returning from his personal reconnaissance the officer commanding was to explain to the leaders of the attacking and bombing parties :-

    (a). The exact point to be attacked.
    (b). The order of the advance and attack.

The following details as regards the method of carrying out the attack were agreed on :-

The centre party was to clear the enemy's trench for a distance of 20 yards on either side of the centre file and was to secure and hold this position.

The right and left parties were not to go beyond the second line German communication trenches: and flanking parties were to bomb outwards.

Thirty minutes after the attacking party left our trenches the Artillery were to barrage certain selected points in the enemy's lines.

The limit of time in the enemy's trenches was to be 20 minutes and the signal for retirement was to be three blasts on a whistle.

The left party was to retire first, followed by the right party and when all was clear, the centre party was to follow.

The O.C. attack was to arrange for a connecting or covering party to be placed half way between the enemy's and our own lines to cover the retreat and pass on wounded and prisoners.

Machine gun fire was to be arranged for at the usual times in order to cover the sound of movement and make the situation appear normal.

All identification marks, letters, maps, etc. were to be left behind by the men taking part in the attack.

3.   Execution.

The raid was carried out according to plan and with very satisfactory results.

In spite of the fact that a low barbed wire entanglement was found in front of the enemy's trench the attacking party succeeded in entering the trench. Bombing at once became general and as the Germans were surprised in their dug-outs, a considerable number of them must have been killed and wounded. A machine gun was destroyed and the party retired with total casualties of one officer and four men wounded.

4.   Summary of remarks by O.C. 4th Battalion Grenadier Guards.

    (a). Duration of time in enemy trench was not enough and should be half an hour at least, in order to give the enemy who run away sufficient time to assemble and counter-attack.
    (b). Bombs were carried in sandbags: it would be preferable to carry them in carriers or buckets provided with covers.
    (c). If the men had life preservers it would be a good thing. The preservers would not interfere with bomb-throwing.
    (d). The enemy's wire at the point of attack was low and proved not to be an effective obstacle against keen men provided with wire-cutters.
    (e). Although the enemy was holding the trench in considerable strength the sudden surprise and bombing attack completely destroyed his nerve and the same operation could have been carried out with less men.
    (f). The enemy's sentries were not alert. The night was dark, cold and stormy.

Adv. First Army.
23rd December, 1915.

4th.Corps.
No.1358/G.

15th.Div.
No.58/G.

15th. Division.

Herewith 4 copies of a report on a bombing expedition, by a party of the 4Bn.Grenadier Guards, N.E. of NEUVE CHAPELLE, on the night of 11th./12th. December 1915.

The G.O.C. considers this a good example of minor enterprise and wishes the copies circulated.

24.12.15.

(sd) P.Stewart Major.
for Brig. General.
General Staff, 4th. Corps.

2.

45th. Infantry Brigade.

One copy herewith for information.

24th. December 1915.

Lieut Colonel.
General Staff, 15th. Division.

IVth Corps No. 1358.(G)

1st Division.
15th Division.
~~18th Division.~~
~~47th Division.~~

Herewith 4 copies of a report on a bombing expedition, by a party of the 4th Battalion Grenadier Guards, N.E. of NEUVE CHAPELLE, on the night of 11th/12th December,'15.

The G.O.C. considers this a good example of a minor enterprise and wishes the copies circulated.

24th December, 1915.

/a. Brigadier General,
General Staff, IVth Corps.

REPORT on BOMBING EXPEDITION south of MAMETZ
(by party of 1st Bn. Cheshire Regiment) on
night of 6th/7th December, 1915.

References to attached sketch map.

The party consisted of 3 officers and 50 men divided into :

    'X' or Advanced Party under Lieut. Harding.

    'Y' or Support Party under Lieut. Harper.

    Reserve or Liaison Party under Lieut. Richardson.

The original intention had been to advance across the crater, but a reconnaissance on the night of the 5th/6th showed that owing to the recent heavy rain, the surface was too sticky. A new line was found leading to a German sap where there was a sniper's post.

At 1-45 a.m. the Advanced Party under Lieut. Harding left the parapet, and at 2-2 a.m. the first bomb was thrown into the sniper's post. It unfortunately did not explode, but a second one killed one of the occupants and wounded another, who, however, unfortunately got away. The party then entered the sap and bombed down to the main trench marked 'C', where a stop was posted at 'D', the remainder of 'X' party turning to the left down the main trench. On the Support Party arriving in the main trench, it was found that the stop at 'D' was being pressed back and had one man wounded, whereupon Lieut. Harper reinforced it and advanced with it to where a communication trench joined it from the left. This stop was able to remain at this point during the whole time the party were in the German trenches, though counter-attacked from 'L' and 'M', and are believed to have accounted for a good many Germans who advanced too boldly down the trenches against them. They were greatly

                                assisted

assisted in this by the West bomb thrower, which threw with great rapidity and accuracy into trench marked 'Q'.

Meantime Lieut. Harding and the advanced party moved along the main trench to their left, killing two Germans at 'E' and killing one and taking one prisoner at 'F'. The latter was sent back to the Liaison Officer at the entrance to the sap. Continuing down the main trench, three dug-outs were discovered and bombed with about half a dozen bombs into each; one was evidently a trench store, but the other two were deep dug-outs believed to contain men, and this was subsequently confirmed by the prisoner taken, who said that the remainder of the guard were in them.

At Point 'G' a stop was put out to the right to point 'H'. Here 'X' party were joined by 'Y' party who continued to bomb down to point 'K' where another communication trench crossed. At this point grenades were running short, as it was found difficult to get fresh supplies from the rear owing to the deep mud in the trenches. A retirement was then ordered and successfully carried out covered by 'Y' party, who picked up the stops as they fell back.

All the party were back in their own trenches by 3-5 a.m.

The West bomb thrower maintained a rapid and accurate fire during the operation. It was placed about point 'A' in our trench to fire into trench 'Q' about point 'M' so as to deal with counter attack on the rear of the party.

100 ball bombs were fired. There were no blinds. The range used was 150 and six second fuze. The bombs burst as they fell and were seen to fall in the German trench. Fire was kept up for about an hour.

A Machine Gun was posted behind 70 fire trench to sweep the slope to the rear of the German trenches, in case they counter-attacked over the top. It was not employed.

The only hitch in the proceedings was owing to the

telephone

telephone instrument, on the way to the sap, becoming so covered with mud that it was unserviceable, and a fresh one was only obtained when the retirement was being carried out.

Most of the German trenches were reported to be in very bad condition, and over knee deep in thick mud. Communication trench 'P', however, was boarded on the bottom, with a drain running underneath, and in good condition. Fire trench 'Q' had large traverses of sandbags with a good slope on them.

Ten Germans were actually accounted for, besides those in the dug-outs, and several more must have been killed or wounded in the counter-attacks on the stops at 'D', 'H' and 'K'.

The casualties were 2 officers very slightly wounded, 1 man severely wounded (since died) and 5 men slightly wounded.

Steel helmets were worn and proved serviceable.

G.H.Q.
18-12-15.

Sketch Map of bombing expedition south of Mametz 6/7 Dec 1915

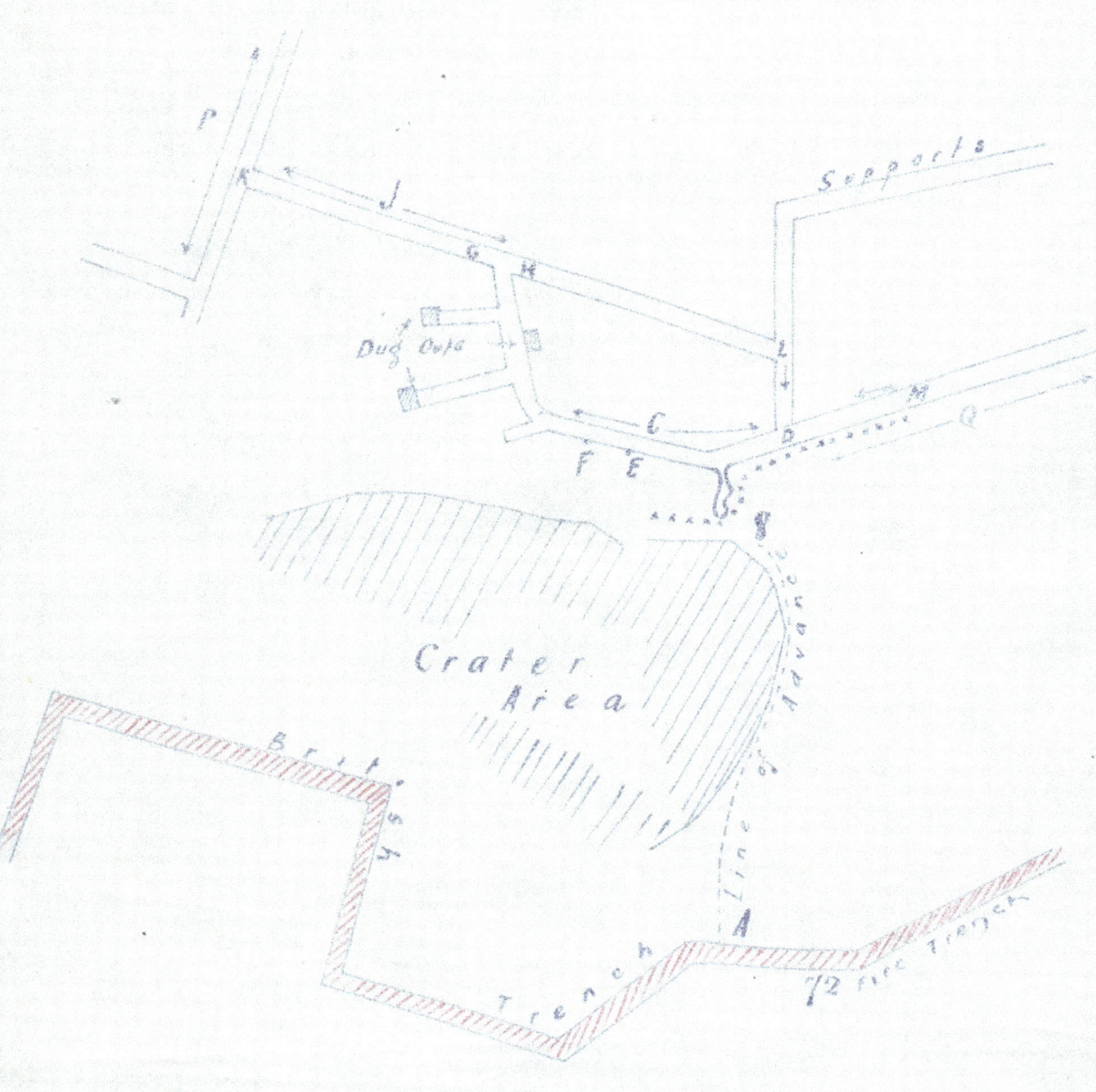

Headquarters
XV Division.

Noted and returned.

T. J. Matheson
Brig. Gen.
Comdg. 46th Inf. Bde.

Dec 1915.

HEADQUARTERS,
15th. DIVISION.
26 DEC. 1915
Reg. No. 1332

1st Army G.S.232.   IVth Corps No. H.R.S. 450

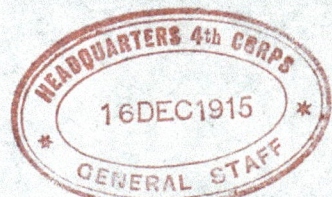

SECRET

IVth Corps.
==========

In continuation of my letter No. G.S. 232 dated 8th December, a further supply of the "Summary of small offensive carried out by the 6th Battalion Gloster Regt" has been received from G.H.Q.

Five additional copies are forwarded herewith in case they may be of use to you.

Adv. 1st Army.   (sd) S.H.Wilson. Major G.S.
                                       for Major General,
15/12/15   General Staff, 1st Army.

(2)

~~1st Division.~~
15th Division.
~~47th Division.~~
~~IVth Corps Arty.~~

One additional copy is forwarded herewith.

16th December, 1915.   /for Brigadier General,
                                     General Staff, IVth Corps.

1 Copy previously received & circulated
10/12/15.

SECRET

Advanced 1st Army.

No. 612 (G) 6.   14th December, 1915.

Reference 1st Army No. G.S. 215/3 (a) para 2:-

1. With the object of :-

   (a) Destroying hostile mineshafts and parapets.
   (b) Causing loss to the enemy.
   (c) Obtaining identifications and prisoners.
   (d) Obtaining information regarding the enemys trenches.
   (e) Lowering the enemy's moral.

   The 2nd Division will carry out the following operations on the 15th/16th instant :-

   (a) A bombardment of the Brickstacks opposite CUINCHY on the morning of the 15th instant.

   (b) An attack by gas along front R.1 (A.27.b.80) to the Canal during the hours of darkness, viz., midnight 15th/16th if wind is favourable. With a view to taking the enemy by surprise, no smoke, rifle, machine gun, or artillery fire will be used simultaneously with this gas attack, and the gas cylinders will all be discharged together.
   If the wind is not favourable, this gas attack will be postponed until after night 16th/17th December, on account of reliefs.

   (c) After the gas attack has been carried out, 5 raiding parties of 1 to 2 Officers and 20 to 30 men each, will move out to explore German trenches with the object of obtaining identifications and prisoners, and information regarding the enemy's trenches.
   If the gas attack has not taken place, patrols will be sent out after dark to ascertain amount of damage done by the morning bombardment.

2. Further operations will be carried out at a later date against the GIVENCHY salient, when gas cylinders have been placed in position, probably about the 23rd instant.

   Details of the scheme of operations will be forwarded later.

   (sd) H.P.Gough   Lieut-General,
                    Commanding 1st Corps.

(2)

~~1st Division.~~
15th Division.
~~47th Division.~~
IVth Corps Arty.

For information.

14th December, 1915.

for Brigadier General,
General Staff, IVth Corps.

1st Army No. G.S.232.

SECRET

1Vth Corps No. H.R.S. 450

[Stamp: HEADQUARTERS 4th CORPS 9 DEC 1915 GENERAL STAFF]

Adv. First Army.

[Stamp: HEADQUARTERS 15th DIVISION 9 - DEC 1915]

O.A.225.

    Herewith 30 copies, Nos. 1 - 30, of Summary of a small offensive operation carried out by the 6th battalion Gloucester Regiment.

    The Commander-in-Chief wishes these circulated as a good example of such minor enterprise.

G.H.Q.   Sd. G.Thorpe. Major G.S.
6/12/15.   for Lieut: General,
                                   Chief of the General Staff.

-2-

1st Division.
15th Division.
47th Division.
1Vth Corps Arty.

Copy No. 17 herewith.

H.Q.1Vth Corps.   for Brigadier General,
9/12/15.   General Staff, 1Vth Corps.

Summary of small offensive operation carried out
by 6th Battalion Gloucester Regiment (48th Division),
on 25th/26th November, 1915.

1. Object of operation.
   (a) To cause loss to the enemy and reduce his moral.
   (b) To obtain information as to enemy's trenches and to secure prisoners.

2. Previous training.
   Thorough reconnaissances of the ground over which the attack was to proceed were made.

   The infantry rehearsed the scheme on a similar portion of our trenches very carefully by day and by night.

3. Scheme.

   Strength of party, five officers, 100 other ranks. Of these, two parties of 25, each under an officer, told off to enter trenches at X and Y on attached plan I. Remaining 3 officers and 50 other ranks to be in support in "Z" hedge at W on plan I. As soon as the two parties are in position 70 yards from German trenches, "ready" to be signalled back to Artillery who commence first barrage, as shown on plan I. The object of this barrage is to make the German sentries take cover, drown the noise of our party approaching, and cutting the wire, and subsequently to prevent German reinforcements coming up from the second line. The first gun to be the signal for the assaulting parties to rush. Bombing parties to be left at each communication trench and the remainder of the two assaulting parties to work to the central point and then retire on to the support. The whole party then to retire to our trenches and second barrage (see plan II) to open to cover retirement.

   A preliminary bombardment by Artillery to take place on the afternoon of the 25th to cut the wire, damage trenches, and attract a working party from whom prisoners are likely to be obtained.

4.

4.   Execution.

Preliminary bombardment, successfully executed by Artillery, at 2-40 p.m. on 25th.

At 11-35 p.m. 90 men of "C" Company, 6th Gloucestershire Regiment, under Captain V. L. Young, left their trenches and reached the "Z" hedge, joining the garrison consisting of Lieutenant H. P. Mott and 20 other ranks who had been there since dark to prevent the Germans occupying it and to keep off any hostile patrols.

The two parties of 25 each, under 2/Lieutenant T. T. Pryce and 2/Lieutenant J. M. C. Badgeley, respectively, moved off at 12-20 a.m.   Owing to bright moonlight they had to move very slowly and reached position of readiness 70 yards from German trench at 12-45 a.m.

Captain Young received reports by telephone at 12-58 a.m. that they were ready to assault.

He waited for a cloud to cover the moon before asking advanced R. A. Officer for No. 1 barrage.   At 1-1 a.m. the signal "ready" was sent back to the Artillery who opened fire at 1-3 a.m. and both parties rushed.

5.   Left Party.   (2/Lieutenant J. M. C. Badgeley).

This party cut through two wire entanglements, the second one being very new, strong, thick wire, 5 yards deep.   The unavoidable noise and delay caused by this gave the enemy sentries the alarm.   2/Lieutenant Badgeley and 10 men got into the trench, 2/Lieutenant Badgeley shot two men and the first dug-out was bombed with two bombs.   The enemy retired then along the trench to left and twelve bombs were thrown at our party, from the parallel in rear.

Touch was gained with the right party, but Lieutenant Badgeley was wounded by a bomb which fell at his feet.   This party then retired, bringing in all their wounded; one of the latter was killed on the way back by a chance bullet.

6.   Right Party.   (2/Lieutenant T. T. Pryce).

This party only found low wire and entered the German trench without alarming the enemy.   The first shelter was a telephone office; one German was just coming up the steps and was called upon to

surrender

surrender. As he did not do so Lieutenant Pryce shot him and the shelter was then bombed with three bombs. A blocking party was established and the N.C.O. in charge pulled up a sump cover which effectually prevented the German supports from reaching our party. Led by Lieutenant Pryce they proceeded down the trench and bombed six shelters in succession. They took 3 unarmed German prisoners; as these were being passed down the trench for evacuation, they darted into a shelter, re-appeared armed, and attacked our party in the rear. They were all killed. Lieut. Pryce, having lost touch with left party, began his retirement up the trench, but found it full of Germans who had apparently reinforced from underground passages. Our party bombed this crowded trench most successfully, climbed out of the trench and retired with all their wounded. The Germans pursued, but were driven back by bombs. Lieutenant Pryce had previously been slightly wounded by a pistol bullet from a German Officer, whom he killed with his revolver. The party safely reached hedge, with the exception of one man who had been sent back with a message to the signallers and was never subsequently seen. One wounded prisoner was brought in by this party.

7. Withdrawal.

Captain Young, having collected the whole of the party at the "Z" hedge, telephoned to the R.A. to stop first barrage, and sent his men back to the trenches in small parties, by pre-arranged routes. Lieut. D.H.Hartog, with rifle grenade party, moved off to the left, and enfiladed the enemy's trench, which was presumably crowded, with twelve rifle grenades. The whole party returned without further casualties.

8. Result of operation.

The raid was most successful, and must have accounted for a large number of Germans, who were caught crowded in big, deep shelters and bombed.

From the prisoner's statement, the garrison at present in the trench was a company 180 strong, of 169th Regiment. 8 Germans were killed in the trench outside the shelters.

The

The success of the enterprise was due to the bravery and keenness of both men and officers, and to the careful previous rehearsing and organization of the parties, full advantage being taken of the information which has been collected and circulated after former attacks.

9. <u>Casualties.</u>

    Killed - 1 man, missing - 1 man.

    Wounded - 2/Lieut. J.H.C.Badgeley,
                2/Lieut. T.T.Pryce.
                18 other ranks.

All the wounded are slight cases, and five are at duty.

10. <u>Composition, formation and equipment of storming parties.</u>

Each assaulting column was formed as under :-

Officer.

4 men with rifles and fixed bayonets.

4 men, each carrying 12 bombs, bludgeon, and bayonet as dagger.

4 men, each with bludgeon and bayonet as dagger.

4 men, with revolvers and bayonets as daggers (for escort to prisoners).

4 men, with rifles and fixed bayonets.

4 men, with 12 bombs each, bludgeon, and bayonet as dagger (these last two sections of fours detailed to block and hold communication trench and point of entry).

2 telephone men, with instrument, to remain at point of entry.

Support party at "Z" hedge.

    3 officers.
    3 grenadiers with rifle grenades.
    50 men in fighting order, with rifles, bayonets, and reserve of bombs.
    1 officer, R.F.A., with telephone and operator.
    3 telephone operators for infantry with 3 instruments.

11. Communications.

Both artillery and infantry had separate new telephone lines, laid from artillery O.P. in our trenches to support at "Z" hedge. Each assaulting party took a telephone and two operators forward, with lines back to two separate instruments at "Z" hedge. Instruments for assaulting party were specially tuned down to buzz quietly. Communications worked perfectly and touch was never lost

12. Bombs.

Amount carried, as detailed on previous page, all no.5. They were all new and freshly detonated. None failed to explode. Grenades were difficult to throw so as to reach the bottom of the deep shelters without lodging on the steps. Some of our men were wounded by splinters from our own bombs. Bombs containing heavy gas would have absolutely prevented the enemy from reinforcing through deep shelters and underground tunnels as they did.

13. Action of Artillery (3rd S.Midland F.A.Brigade).

An artillery officer with a signaller accompanied the Company Commander to the "Z" hedge and was in touch with the R.A. Commander throughout the operations.

The word "ready" was received and fire on lines of first barrage, open at rate of section fire five seconds, at 1-3 a.m.

At request of infantry company commander, at "Z" hedge, this quick rate was kept up till 1-10 a.m. then slowed down to section fire 20 seconds, and at 1-12 a.m. to section fire 30 seconds. At 1-13 a.m. "stop" was received from forward officer and barrage ceased.

At 1-14 a.m. second barrage asked for by R.A. F.O.O. under orders of the company commander. This message was received through both artillery and infantry telephones and

order

order sent to the Battery, but almost immediately "stop" was received from the F.O.O. and transmitted to Battery.

At 1-20 a.m. first barrage again asked for and opened. This was kept up till 1-29 a.m. when "stop" was received.

Artillery stood by ready to open second barrage, but this was not asked for and at 2 a.m. infantry reported "all in".

The barrage seemed to be well maintained and effective. Telephone communication between F.O.O. and Brigade Commander and through Battery Commanders to Batteries worked without a hitch. No. of rounds fired throughout the operations by 3 Batteries :- 340 shrapnel.

Retaliation by enemy's artillery was slight and rather dilatory and was mostly directed at our front trenches. Fifty to sixty rounds from field guns from direction of LA LOUVIERE and howitzers from direction of BOIS du BIEZ were fired into section "K" between 1-30 a.m. and 2 a.m.

14. Artillery barrages.

1st phase.

An R.A. officer and signaller will accompany the infantry company commander to the "Z" hedge and be in communication with R.A. Brigade Commander.

As soon as infantry send back word that the two parties are ready to rush in, the artillery will open fire, forming the barrage of the 1st phase.

A quick rate of fire will be maintained for the first 30 seconds, after which a slower rate of fire will be kept up on the same line, till information is received that the infantry have got back to the "Z" hedge.

2nd phase.

The barrage of the 2nd phase would be formed if and when the infantry require it.

Barrage for First Phase "Attack"
PLAN I

2nd Battery (4 Guns)
Nos. 4, 3, 2 and 1

Gommecourt Wood

1st Battery (2 Guns)
Nos. 4 and 3

"Z" hedge

W

Telephone

O.P.F.
Bde Comdr
O.P.G.

3rd Battery (1 Gun)
No. 4

HEBUTERNE

Front Line of Sector "K"

REFERENCE
① Barrage for First Phase "Attack"
— German Trench

Barrage for Second Phase "Withdrawal"

PLAN II

1 Battery (4 Guns)
Nos 4 to 3, 2 and 1

OPF •
Bde Comd ⊙
OPC •

Front Trench Sector "K"

REFERENCE
① Barrage for Second Phase Withdrawal
⸺ German Trenches

1st Army No.G.S.189.   lVth Corps No. R.H.N.S. 535.

~~1st Division.~~
15th Division.
~~47th Division.~~

        Herewith a copy of a memorandum prepared by the Field Marshal, Commanding-in-Chief, No. O.B./897 dated 5th October, 1915, for your information.

H.Q.lVth Corps.   Brigadier General.
7th October, 1915.   General Staff, lVth Corps.

O.B./897.

Copy No. 4.

MEMORANDUM on the lessons to be drawn from the recent offensive operations.

Exhaustion of troops in attack.

1. If it may be said that we are able to deduce any one lesson more clearly than another from our experiences throughout the campaign it is that the extra power conferred on the defence by the most modern weapons, and the tax on the resources of the attacker both in personnel and material, combine to place a distinct limit to the lasting power and endurance of each separate effort.

It seems to be inevitable that the effect of a preparatory artillery bombardment, even when assisted by a successful flotation of gas, spends itself after a certain time, and enables even a conquered and retreating enemy to rally, entrench and engage in counter attack.

It is only those Corps and Divisional Commanders immediately directing the attacks who can determine when this period has been reached in their respective areas, and it is then incumbent on the superior commander who is co-ordinating the attack to take measures to secure the ground he has won, and commence to re-organise his troops and husband his resources for a fresh effort at the earliest available moment.

2 ../

Local counter-attack to regain ground lost.

2. It nearly always happens that some of the enemy's counter attacks are more or less successful and that, whilst the main fruits of the victory are kept fully secured, certain points of vantage (such as Fosse No.8) are retaken.

Very valiant attempts are often made by energetic divisional and brigade commanders to retake these places before they can be supported by a sufficiently powerful artillery bombardment, and therefore these gallant efforts generally fail, with a certain loss of men and expenditure of ammunition.

I am of opinion that as a general rule these isolated attempts should be discouraged.

I have frequently pointed out the futility of a local counter attack which is delivered several hours after the enemy has seized a line of entrenchments, and it seems to me that such efforts as have been made in the last few days by the 28th Division, although most valiant and determined, have been subject to the same disabilities, and have consequently failed.

Securing tactical localities won.

3. I wish to impress upon corps and divisional commanders the necessity for garrisoning captured points of tactical importance, such as Fosse No. 8, by the best and most ~~avail~~ reliable available troops, and of taking immediate steps to place them in a state of defence (F.S.R. Part 1, Sec. 105,5). Such points are quite certain to be subjected to most severe counter attacks, and it is of the utmost importance to retain possession of them.

Therefore../

Therefore untried troops should not be used for the purpose if it can be avoided.

Artillery Organization.

4. Our artillery organization at the present time is designedly elastic, and it is necessary to arrange the grouping of the batteries and the chain of command to suit the character of each operation. In doing so it is essential to ensure a chain of artillery command that corresponds to the ordinary chain of the command of formations, divisional, corps and army, so as to avoid as far as possible divided responsibility and the serving of two masters. It is also essential to ensure as far as possible that the artillery supporting the action of a formation is under the direct control of the commander of that formation. The co-ordination of the action of the artillery between neighbouring formations is the work of the commander of the next highest formation.

That the application of the above principles is no easy matter is fully recognised, but the success of the artillery action will depend largely on the solution arrived at.

Character and duration of the artillery preparation.

5. When forming a plan of attack the character and duration of the artillery preparation should receive the most careful consideration and should be suited to the object to be attained. It cannot be said that the high road to success is by means of either a short "hurricane" bombardment or a protracted bombardment. The artillery preparation

is designed .../

is designed to achive a certain purpose, namely, to enable the infantry to enter and penetrate the enemy's position, and to do this his works and the obstacles protecting them must be adequately destroyed and his morale shaken. The character of the bombardment must therefore depend on the strength of the enemy's works and the general nature of the plan of attack. If the supply of ammunition permits it is perfectly legitimate to endeavour to deceive the enemy by a bombardment over a more extended front that it is intended to attack. If, however, such attempt at deception were to lead to the dispersion of guns and the distribution of their fire to an extent that would prejudice the effect of the preparation at the point of attack through failure to obtain sufficiently concentrated effect, the main object will be defeated. The first essential is to produce the desired effect.

Counter-batteries.

6. The task of keeping down the enemy's artillery fire is one of supreme importance and difficulty. The co-operation of the artillery with the Royal Flying Corps for this purpose continues to improve, but Army Commanders should consider most carefully the possibility of making this co-operation closer still. Experience has also shown that the above task cannot be allotted exclusively to guns. The heavy howitzers (8-inch and 9.2-inch) must bear their share in it.

Staff Duties.

7. The assembly on the front of attack of the number of troops required to break through the enemy's front necessarily causes great congestion. When to this is added the movements necessary for the supply of ammunition, food and entrenching material to the troops and for evacuation of wounded the difficulty of control becomes serious. However elaborate and carefully thought out the arrangements made beforehand may be, nothing can replace the active personal supervision of staff officers. This is particularly necessary in the higher staffs where new formations are concerned. The expansion of the Army makes it increasingly difficult to provide experienced and well trained staffs, and it can no longer be assumed that measures which would as a matter of course have been taken in our regular divisions in the earlier stages of the war, will now always be carried out efficiently.

Grenades.

8. On the occasion of my visit to Corps and Divisional Headquarters during the operations last week, I received frequent complaints as to the inferiority of our troops in grenade throwing and also as to the inadequate supply of the grenades themselves. I must remind Corps and Divisional Commanders that in my personal interviews with them during the past months I have laid the greatest emphasis on the value and necessity of training as many men as possible in the use of hand grenades. It is not sufficient that a small proportion only of

the men.../

the men in a battalion should be trained as grenadiers and treated as a battalion unit. Every platoon must be prepared to carry out a grenade attack. Moreover, it is not only in throwing the grenade that instruction is required. The organization of "grenadier parties" must be studied, and methods of conducting a grenade attack in trenches must be practised. The replenishment of the supply of grenades to those parties is another most important item and a definite system of effecting it, capable of modification to suit varying conditions, must be carefully elaborated.

Although there has been no lack of grenades in the aggregate, I am aware that we have not yet attained an adequate supply of the types of hand grenade which it is desired to standardize, such as the "Mill's", and this is a matter which is receiving constant attention both at General Headquarters and at the War Office.

Gas Helmets.

9. In the casualty clearing stations I found several cases of gas poisoning amongst our own men, and I am given to understand that in some instances the prescribed precautions against gas have not been observed when there was a necessity for them. It must be impressed on all battalions and company commanders that owing to variations in the wind and to the tendency of gas to hang in hollows and depressions in the ground these precautions are just as necessary

when gas.../

when gas is used on our side as when there are indications of its use by the enemy. Neglect to observe these instructions may not only cause unnecessary losses, but thereby neutralise the chances of success arising from a carefully prepared "gas attack".

General Headquarters.

October 5th, 1915.

Sd. J.D.P.FRENCH.
F.M.
C.-in-C.

1st Division.
15th Division.
47th Division.
================

     Herewith extracts from a report by the G.O.C. 6th Division, and from a report and Operation Order by G.O.C. 16th Infantry Brigade in connexion with the operations at HOOGE in August, 1915.

H.R.S 393

30th August, 1915.

Brigadier General,
General Staff, IVth Corps.

15th Div Art.
15th ~~Div Squadron~~ ADMS
44th Inf Bde
45th Inf Bde
46th Inf Bde

(minute as above)

31st August, 1915

Lieut Col GS

EXTRACT FROM REPORT BY G.O.C. 6th DIVISION, IN REPLY
TO QUESTIONS ASKED BY 2nd ARMY.

1. <u>Close co-operation of Artillery F.O.Os. with the Infantry. Where were the F.O.Os. placed during the various phases of the attack.</u>

(a) Each Infantry Brigade was supported by its own Artillery Brigade.

The positions of the detached officers were as follows :-

    (i) 1 Subaltern from Right Artillery Brigade with H.Q. 2nd Durham L.I.

    (ii) 1 Subaltern from Left Artillery Brigade with H.Q. 2nd York & Lancaster Regiment, but in close touch with H.Q. 1st Shropshire L.I.

    (iii) 1 Captain from each Artillery Brigade with H.Q. Infantry Brigade.

    (iv) 1 Captain per Artillery Brigade at a selected point in rear of firing line acting as General Observing Officer for his Artillery Brigade.

    (v) 1 Officer per Battery at the Battery Observation Station.

These officers had no orders as to changing their positions.

The officer attached to Battalion H.Q. had orders not to go in front of Battalion H.Q. unless expressly instructed to do so by the Battalion Commander.

In any case, no wire was run out in front of Battalion H.Q.

As soon as the bombardment starts, it is impossible

to observe /

to observe anything from an Artillery point of view, and Observation Officers as such were no use. Any observation that could be done later was done by (iv) and (v), who remained in their set positions all day. They could only observe after the attack had taken place.

Officers (i), (ii) and (iii) are purely liaison officers, and did excellent work in letting the Artillery H.Q. know how the Battalions in front line were situated, and in forwarding the requirements of these Battalion Commanders. F.O.O. is, under the circumstances, a misnomer.

2. <u>What were the arrangements made for the bombing parties.</u>

(e) Each platoon had its own Grenade Squad of 7 men, consisting of :-

    1 Bayonet Man.

    2 Throwers)
) all equally trained as throwers.
    4 Carriers)

The Carriers carried 40 grenades, 10 each man, and both Carriers and Throwers were armed with a leaden headed knobkerrie. Of the smaller kinds of grenades, a Carrier can take a double load of 20, and in future the Squads will carry 80 grenades instead of 40. Practically every man in a platoon is ready and trained to take his place as Bayonet Man in a Platoon Squad. These Platoon Squads are an integral part of the Platoon and work with it.

It was found that one squad was sufficient for each communication trench, supplemented by extra carriers.

The /

The fresh supply of grenades was in all cases not quick enough. Carriers should be ready to go up at once to a captured position, and a regular supply each hour or half hour after that. If squads have to work up long communication trenches, extra carriers must be attached, and these need not necessarily be trained grenade men.

It is not considered possible to employ larger squads than the Platoon Squad, which have proved very handy.

All Grenadiers should be taught how to use German grenades. Great use was made of German Grenades by nearly all our parties.

6th Div.No. G/6/22.

6th Corps.

A few points brought out during the late operations at HOOGE may be of interest and are therefore forwarded.

1. I ordered the captured line to be wired as soon as possible. This was done by the R.E. in most gallant manner directly after the position was captured, but with too great a loss in officers and men. I consider it a mistake to wire at all before nightfall. It is costly in men, it marks our position, it advertises the fact that we do not mean a further advance, and it is unnecessary in the present state of German troops, and the efficiency of our Artillery barrage.

2. I gave a definite line to be made good. This appeared to me necessary as a further advance towards the Lake would have led the troops into low ground, and where connection with our former line was long and difficult. At the same time I am convinced that more ground could have been gained. The opportunity for such extension on both flanks could only have been seized by some one in authority on the spot, if the Fort 13, Q.5, Q.8 line, and the BELLEWAARDE position had been previously prepared for assault, the wire cut, and assaulting troops ready. It is of course doubtful whether sufficient Artillery was present to prepare a length of front of such an extent, but it seems clear that at any rate wire should be cut for some distance on both flanks of the actual line to be assaulted, and the Heavy Artillery, less counter-batteries, prepared to ~~run~~ turn all their fire on to one, or both flanks as soon as the original objective is seen to be in our possession.

3. The tendency is to have too many men on the captured

position /

position, caused (1st) by the need for bringing enough weight to crush any opposition which may be met, and (2nd) by the augmentation of the fighting line by carrying parties. It is essential to thin out the line as quickly as possible directly the position is captured, otherwise every shell tells.

4. It is important to observe the fall of the enemy's shell fire for some days previous to the assault, in order to clear those areas of troops on the day of assault as much as possible. Where this was done little loss was suffered; where it was neglected much was incurred.

5. There was much waste of bombs due to unaimed fire, and to faulty methods of carrying bombs. Better training, and better contrivances will meet the case.

6. A large supply of water should be stored as close as possible to be sent up at once.

7. Some special strong dug-outs near the battle field for wounded to crawl into would save lives, and these should be close to exits of recognised communication trenches.

8. More Medical Officers should be attached to assaulting battalions.

9. The removal and burial of the dead, and supply of quick lime as early as possible, needs special arrangements.

10. The anti-shrapnel helmets were considered effective, and saved many men from nasty wounds; but they must be made more distinctive than they areat present for their shape and colour, i,e, a slate blue, now lead to their wearers being fired at by our own men. This actually happened on several occasions.

14th August, 1915.

Major General.
Commanding 6th Division.

16th INFANTRY BRIGADE.

EXTRACT FROM
REPORT ON THE OPERATIONS AT H O O G E 9th AUGUST, 1915.

* * *

(4) Our own bombs were most effective, and both battalions also picked up and used the German bombs freely.

Our men appear to have used a great many bombs without seeing a good target for them; consequently both battalions ran short at times.

A great many bombs were dropped or fell out of the boxes, which are cumbersome.

It is suggested that bombers should carry nothing but bombs and a slung rifle or a revolver.

The supplying of bombs to the firing line was difficult, and the positions of reserve depots required thinking out. The system of supply of bombs to the firing line required to be more organised.

Very large reserves of bombs are suggested.

Probably what is most required is a better carrying apparatus in order to avoid bombs falling out all over the place; and also more definite superintendence of the throwing of bombs. Undoubtedly large numbers were wasted by being thrown at nothing, and by being used at times when rifle fire would have been more effective.

(5) The wires between battalions and the Brigade Headquarters were broken at once.

* * *

(6) Both battalions agree as to the efficacy of the shrapnel helmets, which saved several men from nasty wounds.

(7) The 1st Shropshire L.I. report that several Germans pretended to be dead, and then got up and shot our men in

the back /

the back after they had passed. These men were dealt with. One man of the 2nd York and Lancaster Regiment was set on fire by an explosive bullet. Clips of reversed bullets were found. The morale of German troops was distinctly bad. They were apparently greatly demoralised by the bombardment.

(8) Each battalion employed two companies in front line and two in reserve.

The advance was made in lines of platoons at about 40 yards intervals.

Morale of our men was all that could be desired. They behaved splendidly under very heavy shell fire.

Officers were able to keep good control.

Men got a little out of hand in their desire to get on further, and some who advanced too far were probably killed by our own barrage.

(9) SOME SUGGESTIONS.
   (a) A larger supply of water must be stored ready to be sent up at once.
   (b) Some special strong dug-outs should be made ready for wounded to crawl back to.
   (c) Stretcher parties were very late in arriving. They should be on the spot immediately it is dark.
   (d) More Medical Officers are required to each battalion going into action. The 1st Shropshire L.I. had an extra one on this occasion. It is suggested that one Medical Officer should be up in the firing line, and a second in the Regimental aid post.

(e) More runners required - to be posted on relay system. Well buried wires would be a help, but in this case there was no time to do this thoroughly.

(f) Sanitary measures to be taken immediately position is held require to be arranged for.

10. In conclusion, I submit the following points with regard to which I think valuable experience has been gained:-

(a) The necessity for disposing supporting troops away from the probable areas of enemy shell fire. As far as this Brigade is concerned, it was recognised beforehand that this area was bounded by the MENIN ROAD - the South edge of ZOUAVE WOOD - OXFORD STREET - and G.H.Q. line back to the MENIN ROAD. This area was entirely cleared, and the supporting troops disposed in the trench running South from the South arm of OXFORD STREET, in the West end of OXFORD STREET, and in HALFWAY HOUSE, suffered practically no loss.

(b) The absolute necessity for good communication trenches. The existing ones were, in my opinion, badly sited and not nearly deep enough or sufficiently protected.

* * *

(c) Where no natural cover exists for Collecting and Dressing Stations, strong deep dug-outs should be constructed some little way off but connected with recognised communication trenches.

* * *

(d) Bombing parties should be supplied with bombs by some system of sending them up from reserves at

regular /

regular intervals to certain points, thus obviating the necessity of sending back for them.

The whole system of bomb carrying equipment requires organization. The boxes at present in use for certain types of bombs are most unsatisfactory.

(6) The question of disposal of the dead in a captured trench which it is intended to hold is one which requires careful previous arrangement. Burial parties previously detailed should start work as soon as possible by day if the situation permits, but in any case as soon as it is dark. Parties should not be too big, each under a selected N.C.O. with an officer to superintend the area. Quicklime should be provided beforehand. Each party should, if possible, be accompanied by a trained R.A.M.C. orderly to minimise the risk of badly wounded men being buried.

*   *   *

EXTRACT FROM 16th INFANTRY BRIGADE OPERATION ORDER
OF 6th AUGUST, 1915.

x   x   x

10. Machine guns and trench howitzers are to be brought up to captured line at once.

11. R.E. Stores of 30,000 sandbags, wire, 400 shovels, pickets, are dumped at southern end of R.12.

12. S.A.A. reserves of 200 boxes S.A.A. have been put at places selected by Commanding Officers, 1/K.S.L.I. and 2nd York & Lancs.

13. Sandbags. Every man will carry four sandbags.

14. Packs will be stored under battalion arrangements.

15. Rations. One day's rations and the iron ration will be carried.

16. Screens. (a) German screens must not be pulled down.

        (b) Yellow screens will be issued and put up to show that troops have gained a certain position and cannot advance further without artillery support.

        (c) Blue and yellow flags will be waved by selected N.C.Os. to indicate to our artillery that our shells are falling short.

        (d) Bombers will mark their progress up trench by yellow and green flags.

x   x   x

18. Battle Police. 1/Leicester Regt. will put battle police -
    (1) at point where OXFORD STREET joins S.6 - S.8.

    (2) at east end of communication trenches Y and Z and of the communication trench on N. of MENIN road.

Duties

Duties of the police are to collect stragglers and send them back to their units in parties. They are to send back any unwounded men who are helping back wounded men. Police to be in position by 2.30 a.m.

x   x

20. <u>Maps and documents.</u> No maps or documents are to be carried by anyone taking part in the attack.

x   x

(Sd) H. Headlam, Capt.,
Bde.-Maj., 16th Inf. Bde.

Issued at 5 p.m. by Signals.

IVth Corps No. H.R.S.

15th Division.
~~47th Division.~~

Extracts from a memorandum issued by the G.O.C. 8th Division on the 27th February, 1915, previous to the attack on NEUVE CHAPELLE, are forwarded herewith for your information.

Brigadier-General,
General Staff, IVth Corps.

H.Q. IVth Corps.
28th August, 1915.

Extracts from memorandum regarding preparations made for operations for the capture of NEUVE CHAPELLE.

1. **Assembly of attacking troops.**

    *   *   *   *

    Rendezvous will be selected where the troops will halt, before moving on so as to be in their covered places of assembly one hour before daylight. The exact hour will depend on the date fixed for the operation.

    1st Line transport will accompany the battalions to the rendezvous, and will then be parked in places to be detailed in Divisional Orders. At the rendezvous troops will have a hot meal and will be issued with two extra bandoliers of S.A.A. per man, and water-bottles will be refilled.

    *   *   *   *

2. **Previous preparations.**

    The troops holding "B" lines will carry out the work of reclaiming our front trenches, cutting steps for the attacking brigades to issue by, and improving existing communication.

    On the night previous to the attack the trench garrison will cut the wire in front of our trenches on the front of attack and saw through the hedge running in front of our trenches between the two roads which pass to the front through "B" lines.

    Commanding Officers, Company, Platoon, and Section Commanders of the attacking battalions will visit the trenches under orders to be issued by Brigade Commanders, and make themselves acquainted with their places of assembly and lines of advance.

    In addition to the above, Brigadiers and Commanding Officers have been instructed to make certain that all ranks are made thoroughly acquainted with the minutest details of the task before them, before leaving billets for the operation.

* * * *

Depots of R.E. stores will be formed in the neighbourhood of the RUE BACQUEROT and the RUE TILLELOY, and additional stores will be placed in dug-outs in rear of the trench line. The details of these are being worked out and will be forwarded shortly.

One day's rations for the attacking brigades will be packed in sandbags and stored in dug-outs in rear of our trenches.

An additional 100 rounds of S.A.A. per man of the attacking brigades will be stored in the neighbourhood of the RUE TILLELOY.

3. Proposals for carrying out the operation in detail.

* * * *

Wire cutting parties will be with the leading line. "Blocking Parties" under an Officer, and each consisting of 3 sappers, an infantry section, a party of grenadiers, and one machine gun, will be previously detailed to block each hostile trench leading from the right flank of the attack. Two such parties will also be detailed for the left flank in case of necessity, and parties will be detailed to work up the communication trenches leading back from the front German trench.

* * * *

During the period of the first bombardment, the troops in the trenches, including those detailed for the assault (who will use trench ammunition only, keeping their own ammunition intact), will keep up a heavy fire on the German wire in their front with rifles, machine guns, and bombs.

Trench mortars/

Trench mortars will direct their fire on the German trenches west of (28) and on the MOATED GRANGE. When the assault goes forward, the fire from the trenches will continue on the flanks of the attack.

4. Miscellaneous points not previously dealt with.

*   *   *   *

Water. Receptacles of Willesden canvas are being made and will be issued to 23rd and 25th Infantry Brigades to carry up water to the captured trenches. The R.E. will make troughs with holes perforated in them to place under pumps in the village so as to fill waterbottles.

Dressing Stations and Regimental Aid Posts.

The details of these are being worked out by the A.D.M.S. Regimental Aid Posts will be established in the neighbourhood of ROUGE CROIX and the RUE DE BACQUEROT.

Dress and equipment.

i. Infantry will carry one ration and the unexpired portion of the day's ration in the haversack. Haversacks will be carried on the back. Packs will not be carried. The greatcoat will be worn, and arrangements will be made by battalions for the skirts of the greatcoat to be fastened back in the French manner to give freedom to the men's legs.

ii. Water bottles to be filled at the Rendezvous.

iii. Two bandoliers of S.A.A. will be issued to each man in the assaulting Brigades (in addition to his equipment ammunition) at the Rendezvous.

iv. Every/

iv. Every man in the assaulting columns will carry two sandbags in his belt, at the back.

Wire-cutters.   Wire-cutters in the Division will be pooled, and issued to the 23rd and 25th Infantry Brigades to increase the present establishment. Additional wire-cutters ans wire-breakers will be indented for.

The wire-cutters will be issued to trained wire-cutting men in each Platoon of assaulting battalions, and must be tied to the man by a lanyard to prevent loss. These wire-cutters must be collected from casualties in the same way as ammunition.

Each Section R.E. will detail a special wire-cutting party in addition, who will be ready to assist wherever battalions are hung up by wire.

Grenadiers.
*   *   *   *

2 men per company in each battalion will be left at the grenade depots in the trenches, to carry up grenades to the captured German trenches during the second bombardment. Similar arrangements will hold good for carrying grenades forward to the village.

Brigade ammunition columns will fill up to 2,000 grenades Divisional Ammunition Column will fill up to 2,000 grenades.

The total grenades required are based on the scale laid down below, but the exact numbers and distribution must depend on the nature of the grenades in possession of Infantry Brigades and available in Artillery Ammunition Columns.

(a) With Grenadiers of each Infantry Brigade
      at least 2,000   = 6,000

(b) In Trench Depots:-

   B Lines - 4 Depots of 500 each - 2,000)
   C Lines   "   "   "   "   "   500)   3,000
   D Lines   "   "   "   "   "   500)

(c) With each Ammunition Column 2,000   =   6,000

                                       Total   15,000
                                              =========

(d) Divisional Ammunition Column:-

   To fill up after issuing all possible to Brigade Ammunition Columns. Bombs expended by Infantry Bdes will be replaced from Brigade Ammunition Columns in the same way and at the same time as S.A.A.